ENGLISH MALAY

VISUAL DICTIONARY

Tuomas Kilpi

OPPIAN

Publisher: Oppian Press
Helsinki, Finland

ISBN 978-951-877-158-9

Table of Contents • Isi kandungan

fork
garpu

knife
pisau

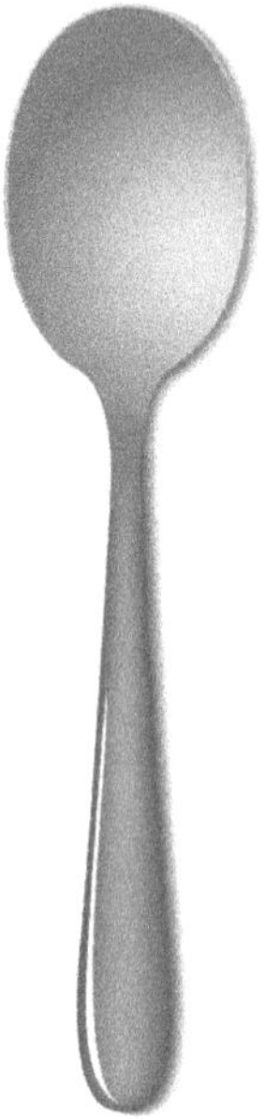

spoon
sudu

plate
pinggan

kettle
cerek

glass
cawan

frying pan
kuali

mug
kole

teapot
teko

strainer
penapis

spatula
sudip

beans
kekacang

rice
beras

potato
kentang

date
kurma

tea
teh

coffee
kopi

apple
epal

pear
pir

banana
pisang

carrot
lobak merah

sweet potato
ubi keledek

garlic
bawang putih

onion
bawang

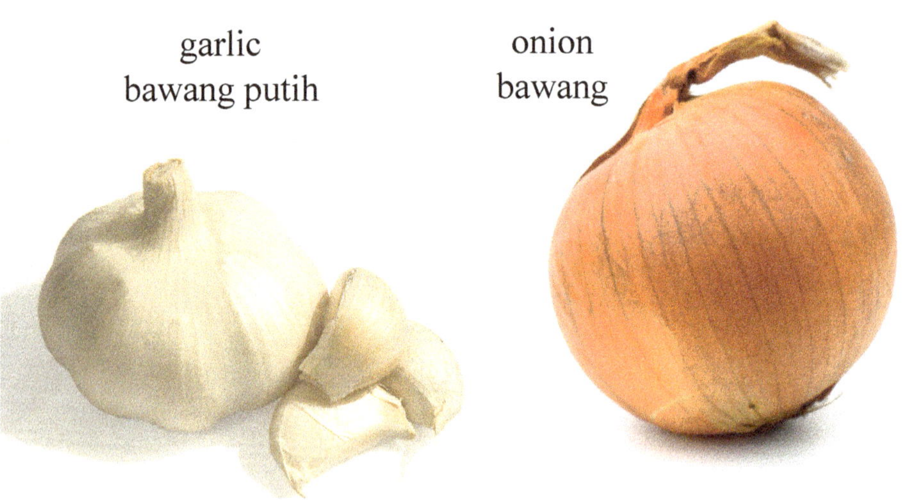

pineapple
nanas

strawberry
strawberi

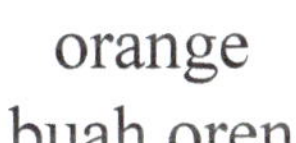

coconut
kelapa

lemon
lemon

kiwi fruit
buah kiwi

tomato
tomato

cucumber
timun

raspberry
raspberi

apricot
aprikot

grapes
anggur

papaya
betik

melon
melon

plum
plum

mango
mangga

watermelon
tembikai

aubergine
terung

fig
buah tin

chili
cili

cauliflower
kubis bunga

turnip
lobak putih

cabbage
kubis

leek
lik

mushroom
cendawan

lettuce
salad

salt
garam

cooking oil
minyak masak

flour
tepung

sugar
gula

margarine
marjerin

milk
susu

cheese
keju

bread
roti

pasta
pasta

ice cream
aiskrim

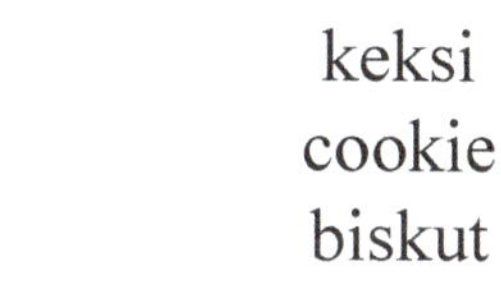

keksi
cookie
biskut

chockolate
coklat

hamburger
hamburger

sandwich
sandwic

candy
gula-gula

pizza
piza

woman
perempuan

man
lelaki

girl
budak perempuan

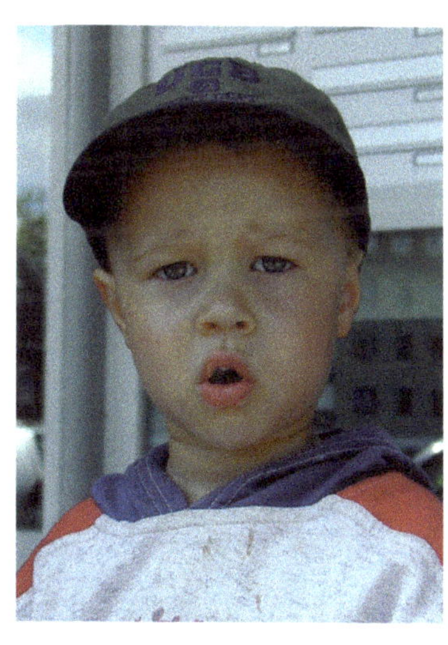

boy
budak lelaki

coat
kot

pants
seluar

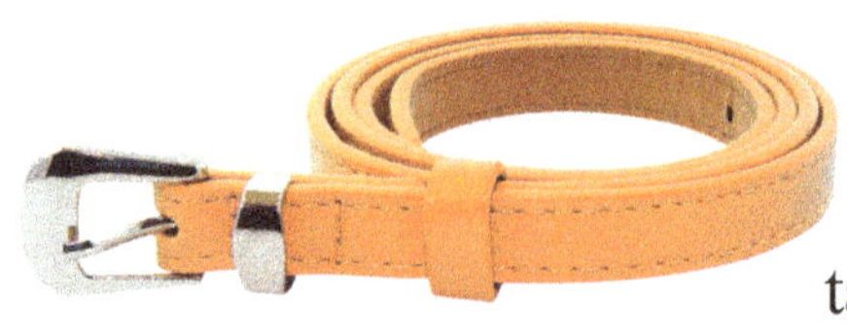

belt
tali pinggang

socks
stoking

shoes
kasut

shirt
kemeja

skirt
skirt

scarf
selendang

boots
but

hat
topi

lamb
biri-biri

cow
lembu

fish
ikan

cat
kucing

pig
khinzir

dog
anjing

chicken
ayam

egg
telur

squirrel
tupai

hedgehog
landak

rat
tikus

hare
arnab

wolf
serigala

fox
musang

moose
moose

bear
beruang

snail
siput

spider
labah-labah

snake
ular

frog
katak

mosquito
nyamuk

wasp
tebuan

nee
lebah

fly
lalat

bathroom
bilik air

kitchen
dapur

bedroom
bilik tidur

living room
ruang tamu

ceiling
siling
window
tingkap
wall
dinding
floor
lantai

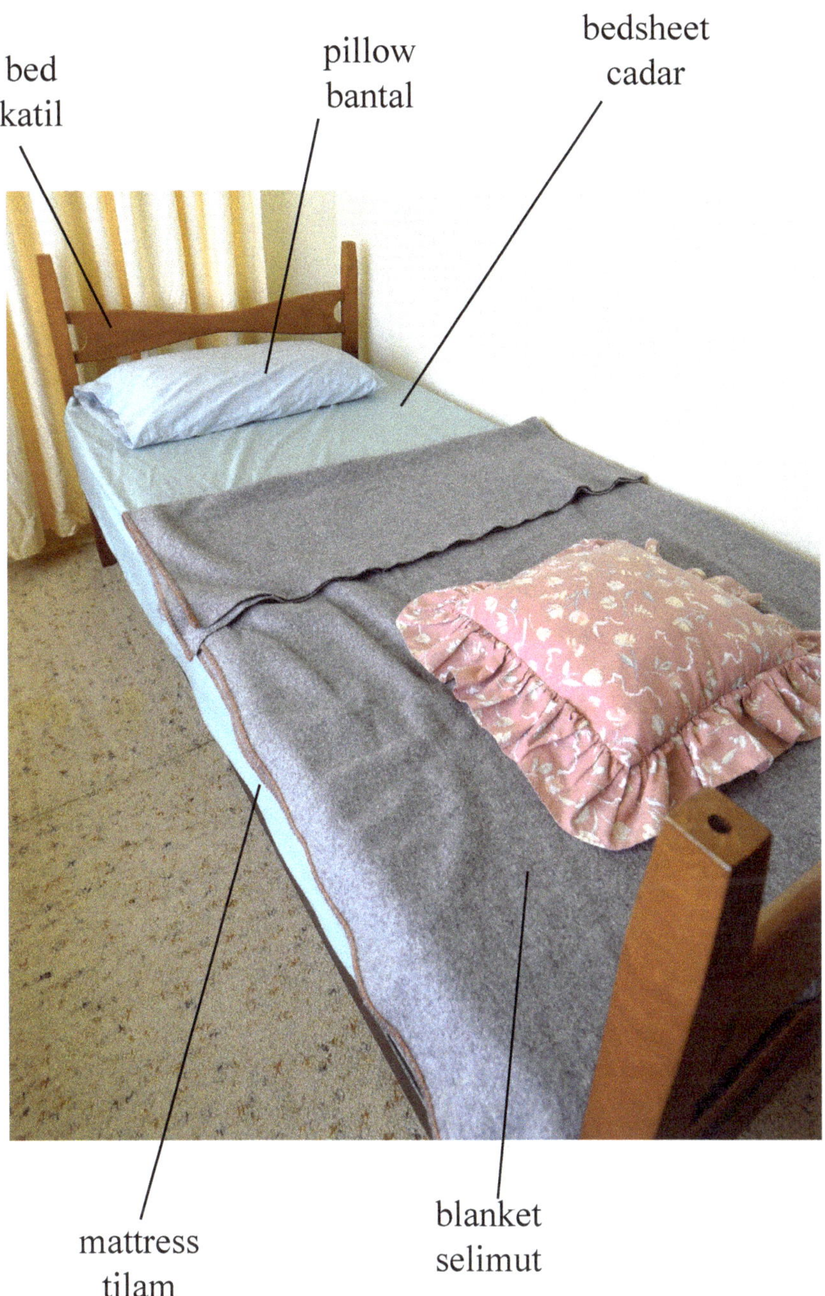

bed
katil
pillow
bantal
bedsheet
cadar
mattress
tilam
blanket
selimut

rug
permadani

lamp
lampu

umbrella
payung

table
meja

chair
kerusi

scissors
gunting

tape
pita pelekat

envelope
sampul surat

parcel
bungkusan

stamp
setem

soap
sabun

toilet paper
tisu tandas

toothbrush
berus gigi

toothpaste
ubat gigi

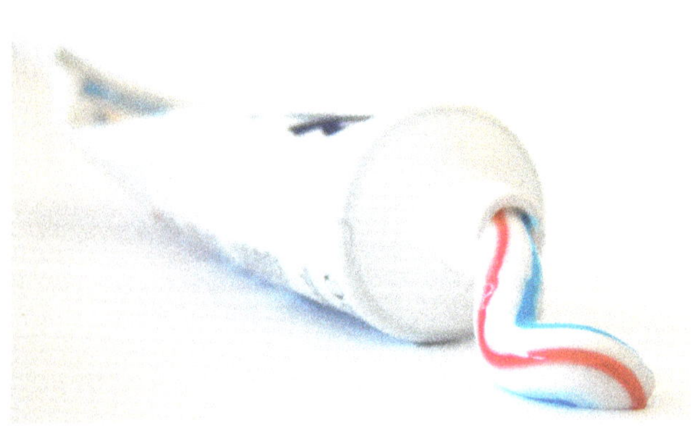

brush
berus

comb
sikat

dental floss
benang flos

deodorant
deodoran

scale
alat penimbang berat

electric razor
pencukur elektrik

television
televisyen

remote control
alat kawalan jauh

mouse
tetikus

computer
komputer

printer
alat pencetak

satellite dish
piring satelit

charger
pengecas

memory stick
pemacu kilat

phone
telefon

shovel
penyodok

rake
pencakar

tape measure
pita pengukur

pliers
playar

saw
gergaji

electric drill
gerudi elektrik

screwdriver
pemutar skru

screw
skru

nail
paku

hammer
penukul

wrench
sepana

credit card
kad kredit

wallet
dompet

banknote
duit kertas

coin
syiling

timetable
jadual waktu

passport
paspor

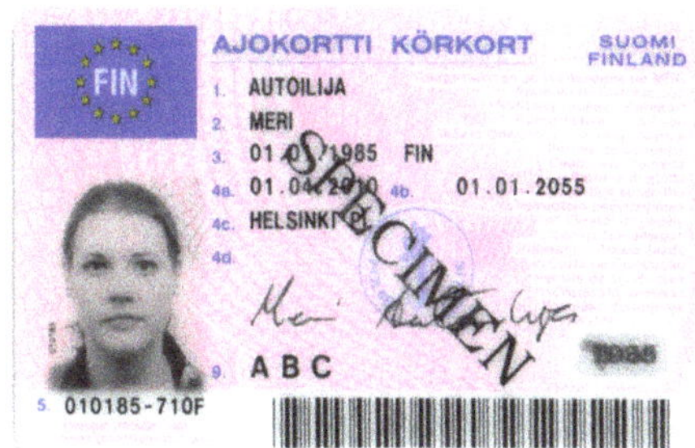

driving licence
lesen memandu

fingerprint
cap jari

jar
balang kaca

bottle
botol

can opener
pembuka tin

bottle opener
pembuka botol

tin can
tin makanan

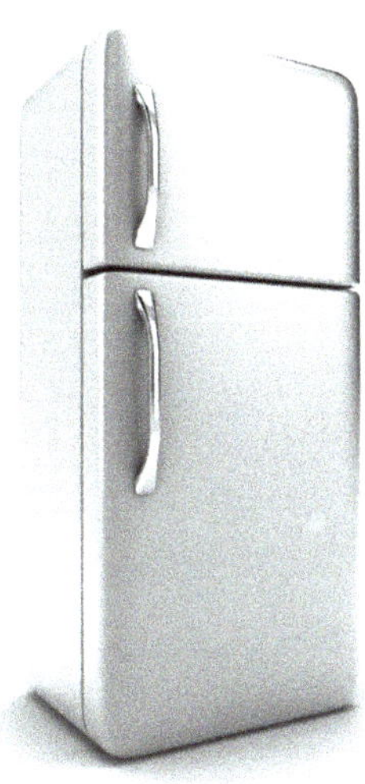

peti sejuk

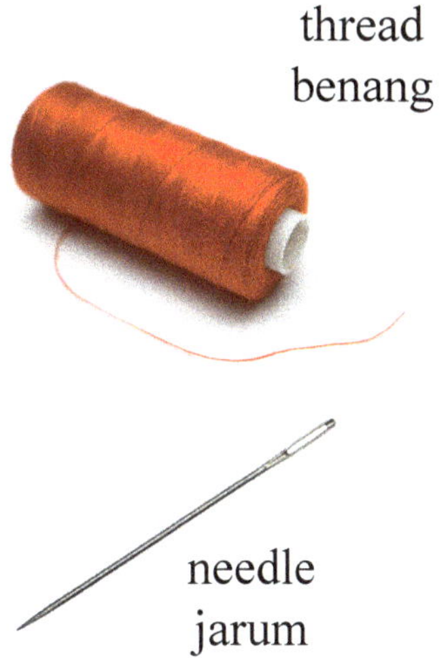

thread
benang

needle
jarum

clothes peg
penyepit baju

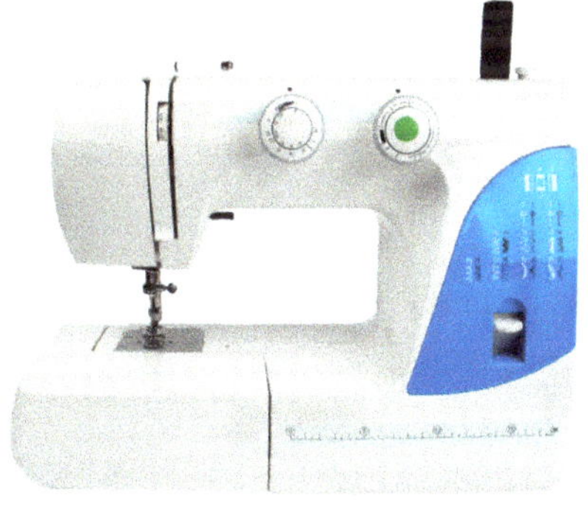

sewing machine
mesin menjahit

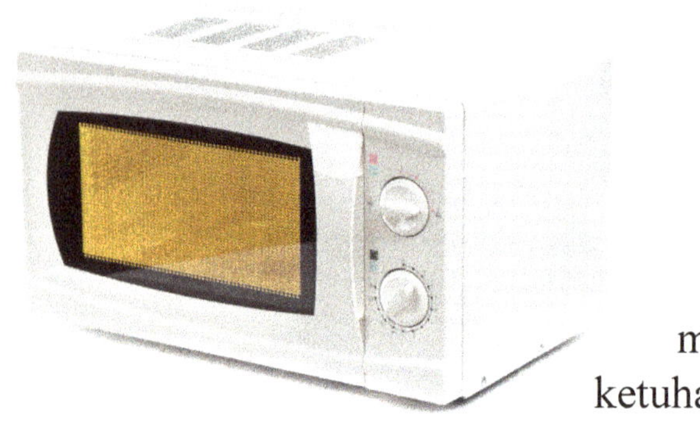

microwave oven
ketuhar gelombang mikro

calculator
kalkulator

stove
dapur

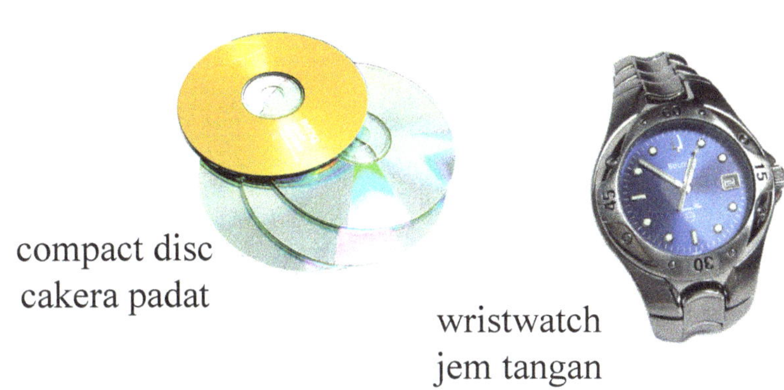

compact disc
cakera padat

wristwatch
jem tangan

radio
radio

fan
kipas

headphones
fon kepala

guitar
gitar

saxophone
saksofon

drum
drum

violin
violin

microphone
mikrofon

bass guitar
gitar bes

mandolin
mandolin

loudspeaker
pembesar suara

book
buku

newspaper
surat khabar

eyeglassess
cermin mata

key
kunci

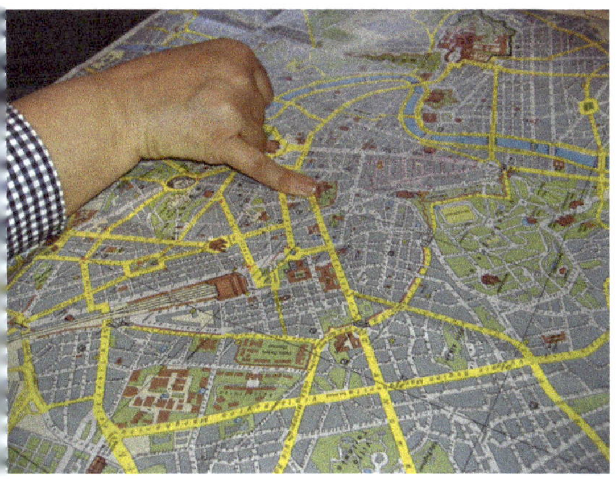

map
peta

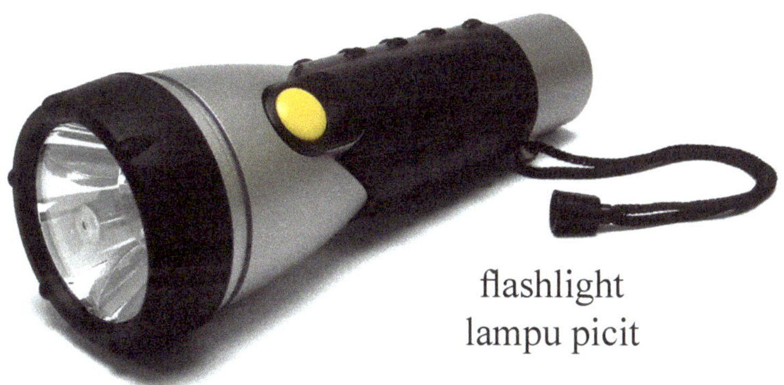

flashlight
lampu picit

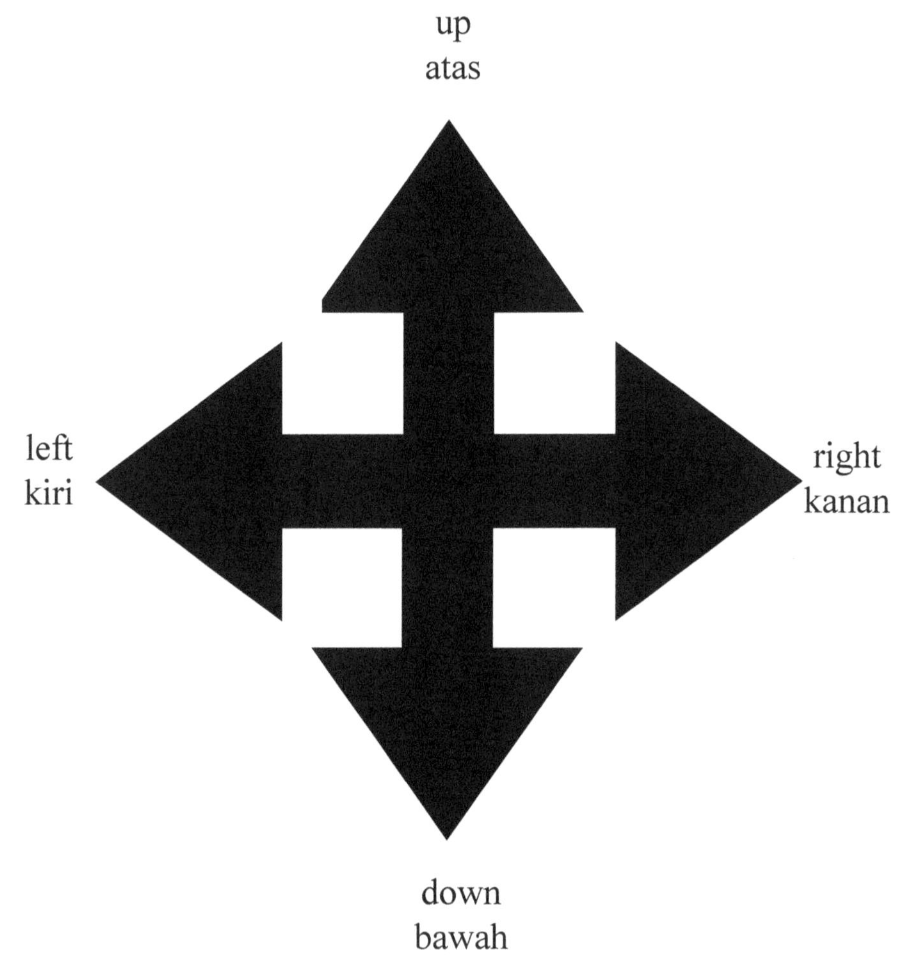

up
atas
left
kiri
right
kanan
down
bawah

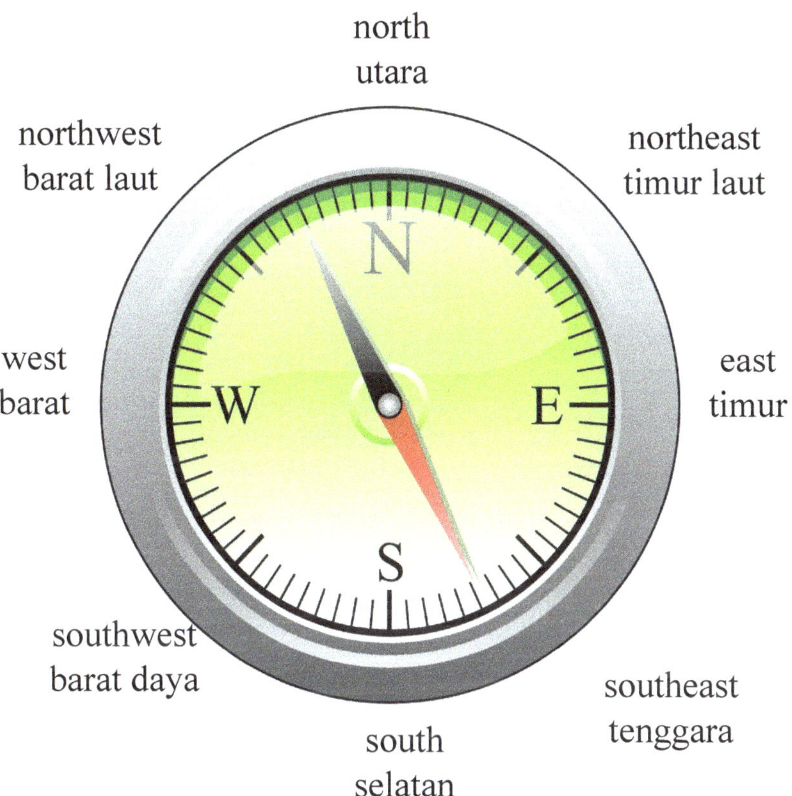

north
utara
northwest
barat laut
northeast
timur laut
N
west
barat
W
E
east
timur
S
southwest
barat daya
southeast
tenggara
south
selatan

shoulder bag
beg sandang

briefcase
beg bimbit

backpack
beg galas

plastic bag
beg plastik

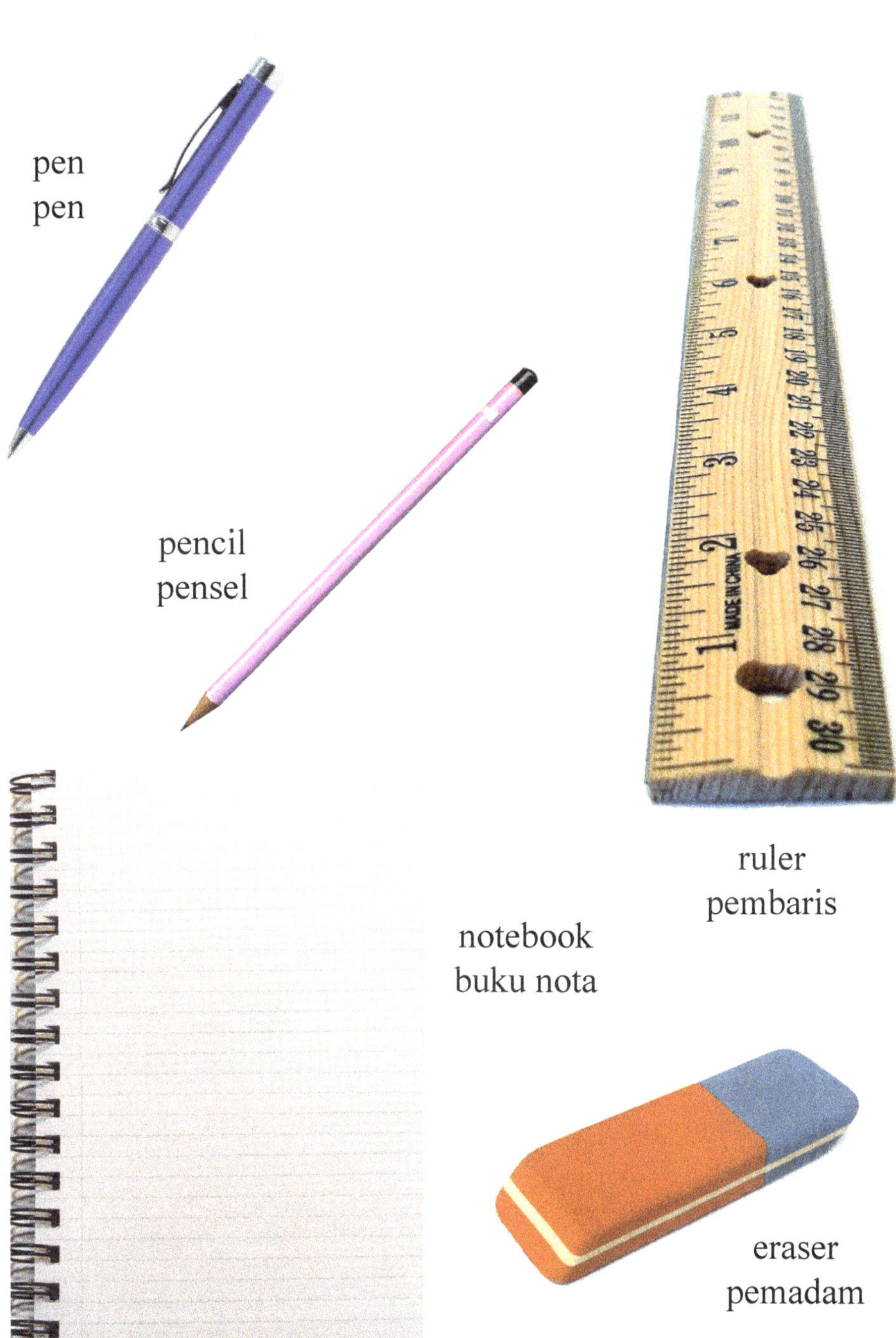

pen
pen
pencil
pensel
ruler
pembaris
notebook
buku nota
eraser
pemadam

car
kereta

bus
bas

van
van

tram
trem

train
keretapi

motorcycle
motorsikal

bicycle
basikal

airplane
kapal terbang

roller skates
kasut roda

tractor
traktor

scooter
skuter

ship
kapal terbang

helicopter
helikopter

truck
trak

snowmobile
kereta salji

traffic lights
lampu trafik

traffic sign
papan tanda

zebra crossing
lintasan pejalan kaki

gas station
stesen minyak

bus stop
hentian bas

vacuum cleaner
penyedut hampagas

dishwasher
mesin pembasuh
pinggan mangkuk

smoothing iron
seterika

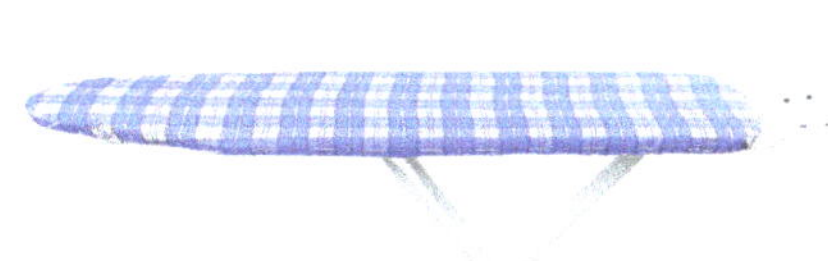

ironing board
papan seterika

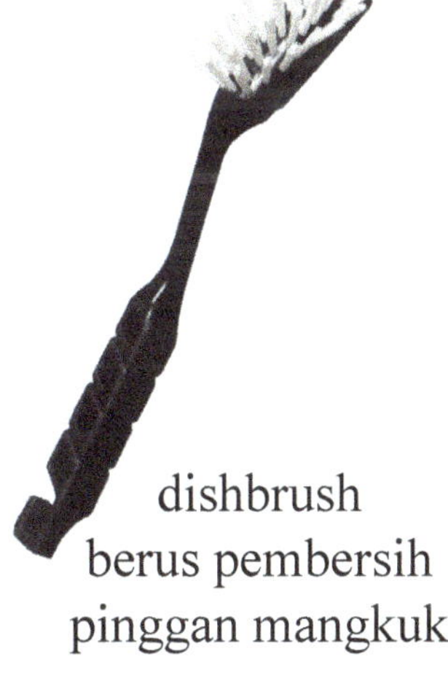

dishbrush
berus pembersih
pinggan mangkuk

washing machine
mesin basuh

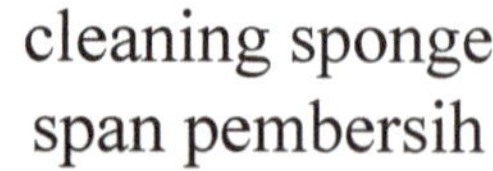

cleaning sponge
span pembersih

puhdistusliina
cleaning cloth
kain lap

mop
pengelap lantai

dusting pan
penyodok sampah

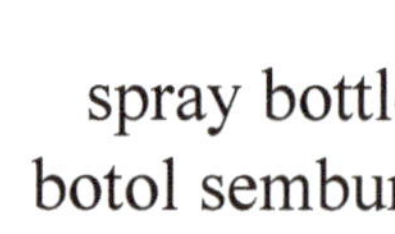

spray bottle
botol semburan

broom
penyapu

bucket
baldi

cot
katil bayi

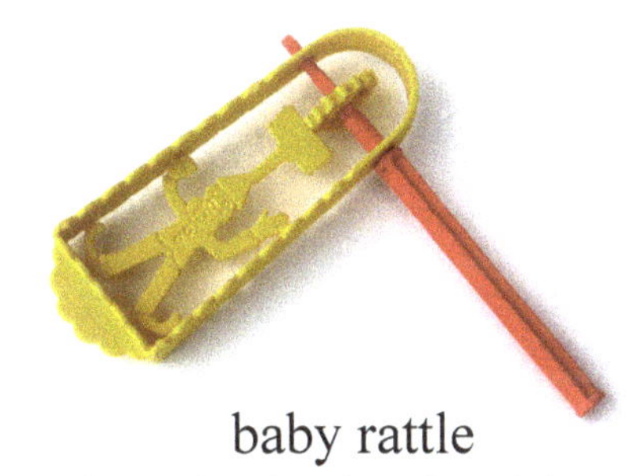

baby rattle
mainan kerincing bayi lampin

diaper
popok

pacifier
puting

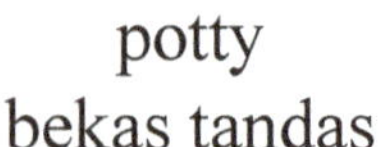

potty
bekas tandas

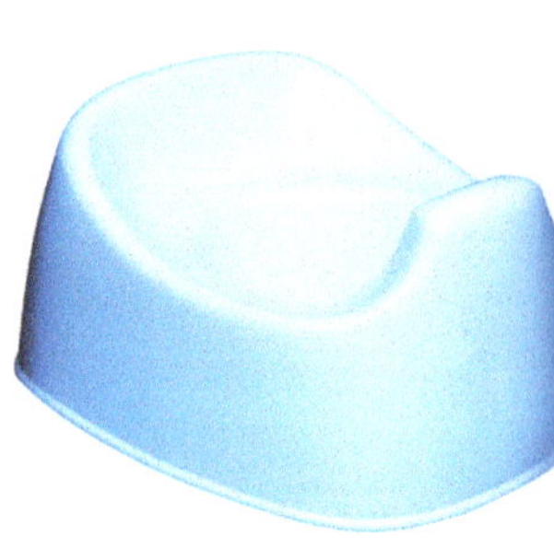

pram
kereta sorong bayi

baby bottle
botol susu

doll
anak patung

football
bola sepak

dice
dadu

kite
layang-layang

game console
konsol permainan

tennis ball
bola tenis

basketball
bola keranjang

ice hockey
hoki ais

puzzle
teka-teki jigsaw

dartboard
papan dart

dart
dart

chess
catur

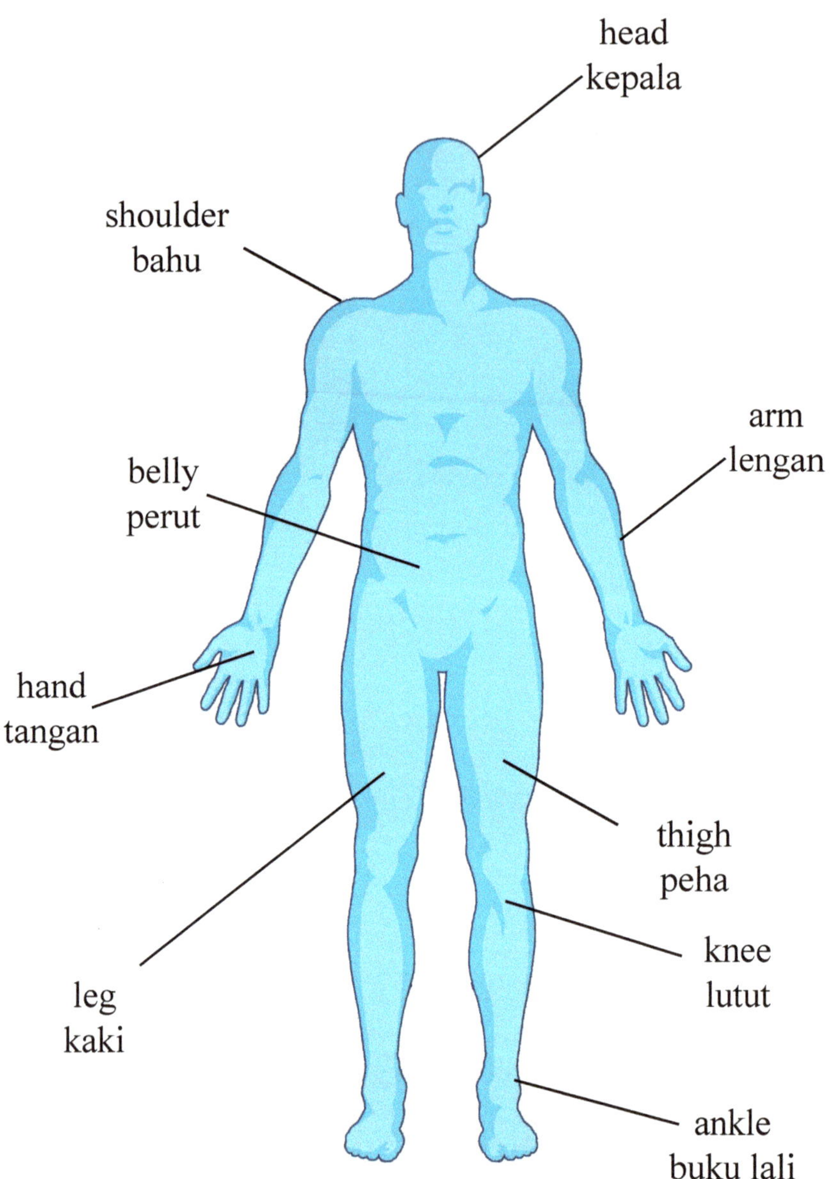

head
kepala
shoulder
bahu
arm
lengan
belly
perut
hand
tangan
thigh
peha
knee
lutut
leg
kaki
ankle
buku lali

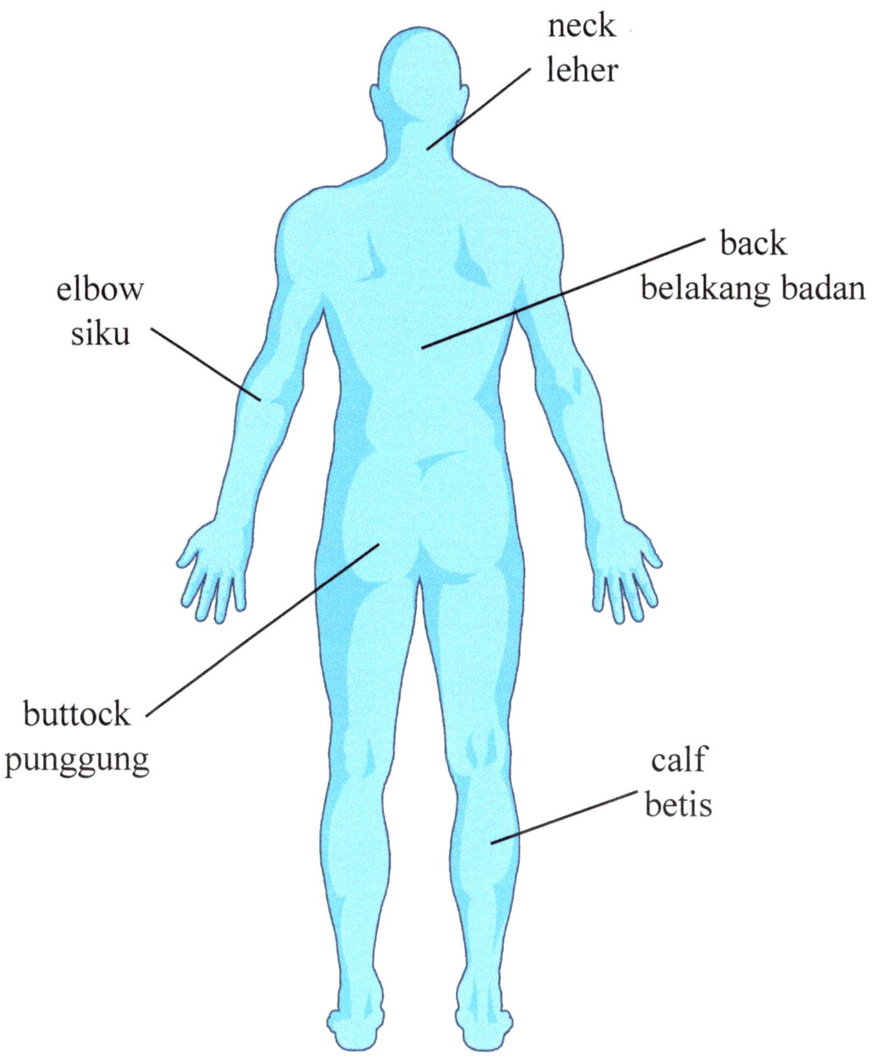

neck
leher
back
belakang badan
elbow
siku
buttock
punggung
calf
betis

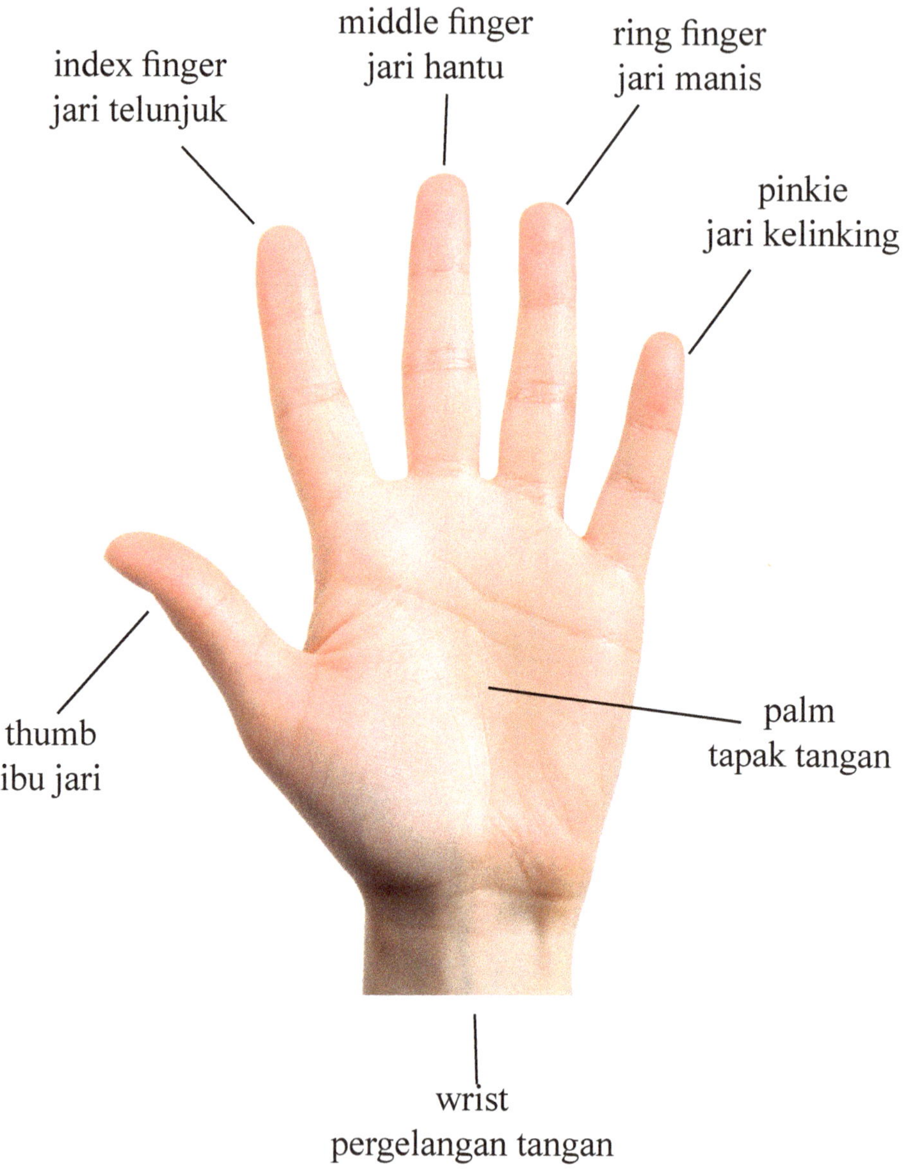

index finger
jari telunjuk
middle finger
jari hantu
ring finger
jari manis
pinkie
jari kelinking
thumb
ibu jari
palm
tapak tangan
wrist
pergelangan tangan

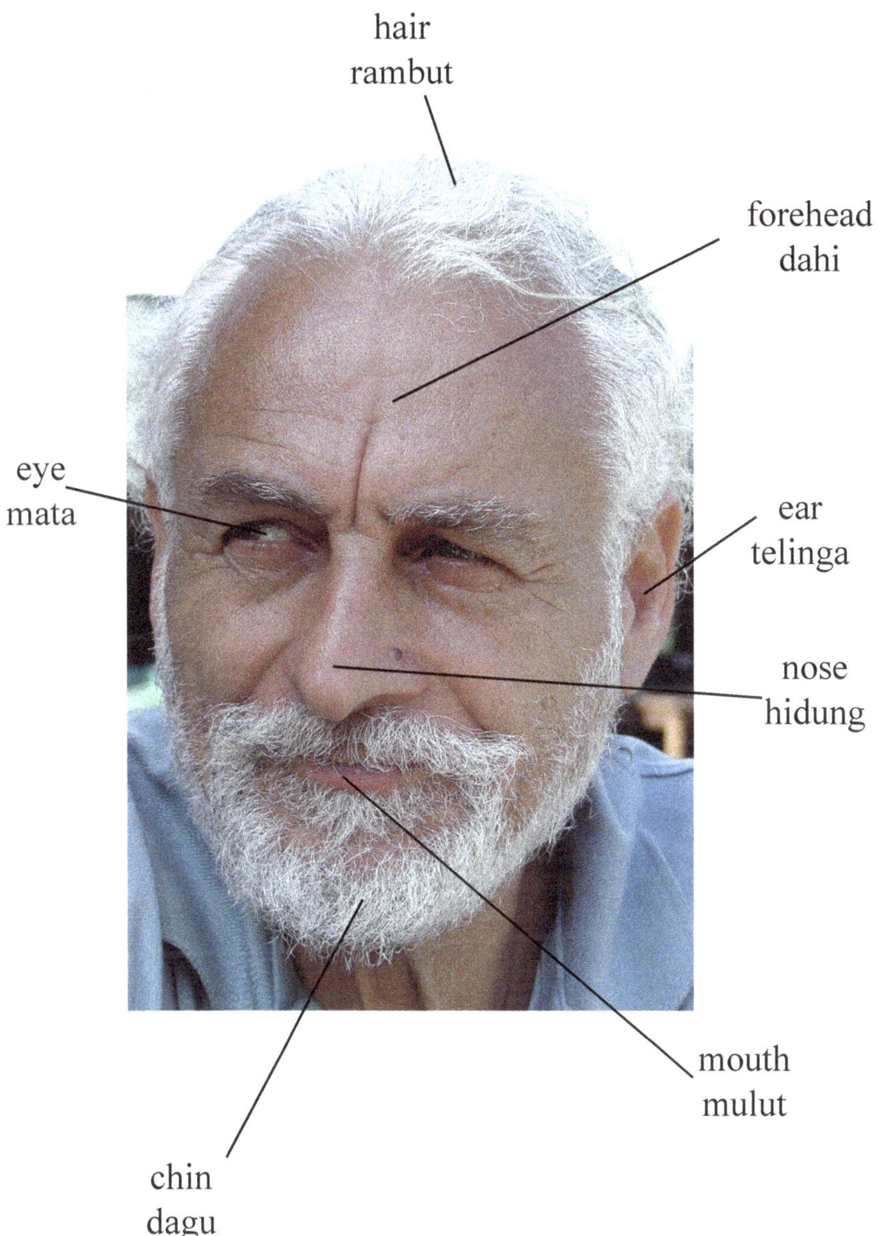

hair
rambut
forehead
dahi
eye
mata
ear
telinga
nose
hidung
mouth
mulut
chin
dagu

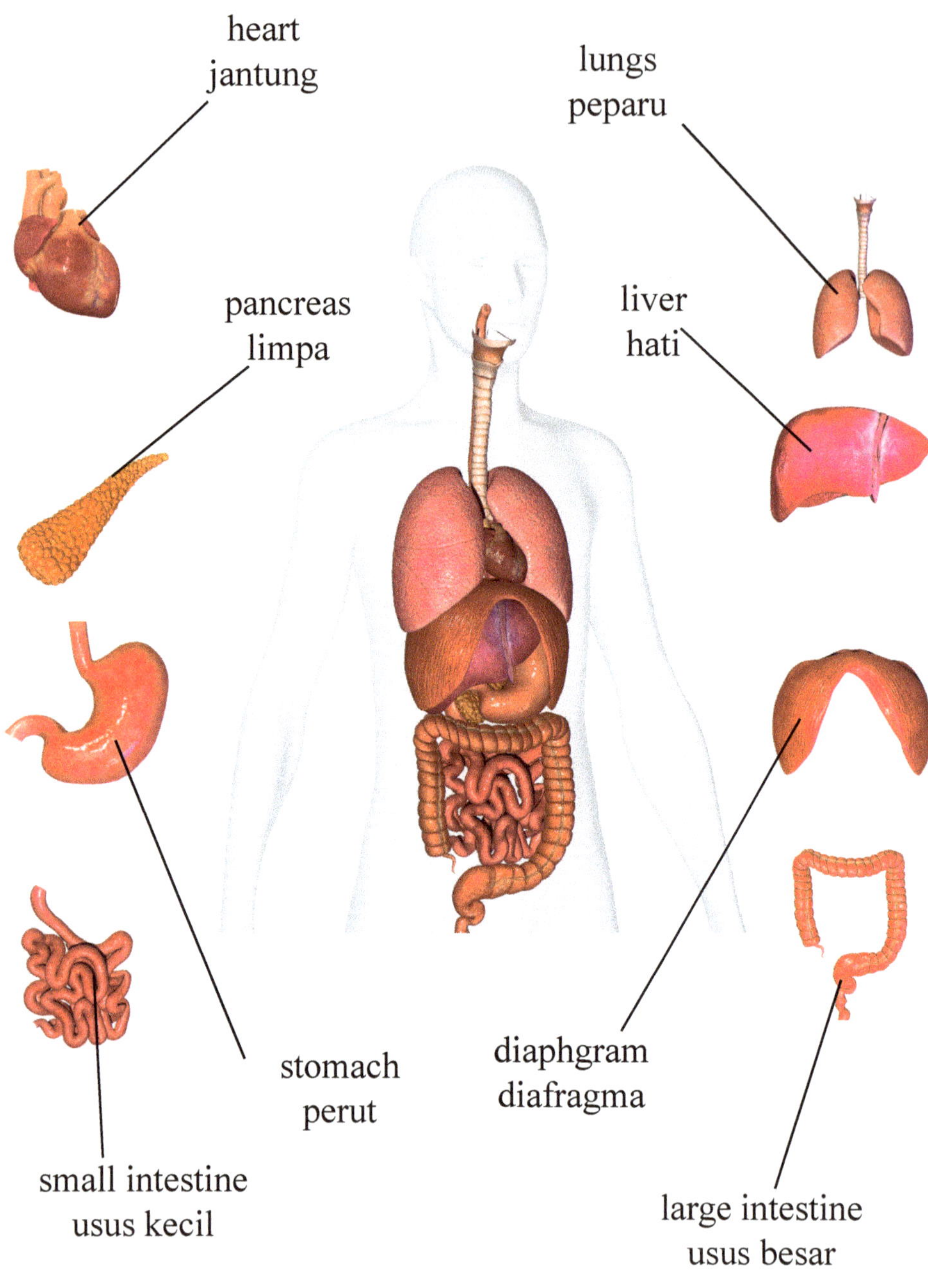

heart
jantung
lungs
peparu
pancreas
limpa
liver
hati
stomach
perut
diaphgram
diafragma
small intestine
usus kecil
large intestine
usus besar

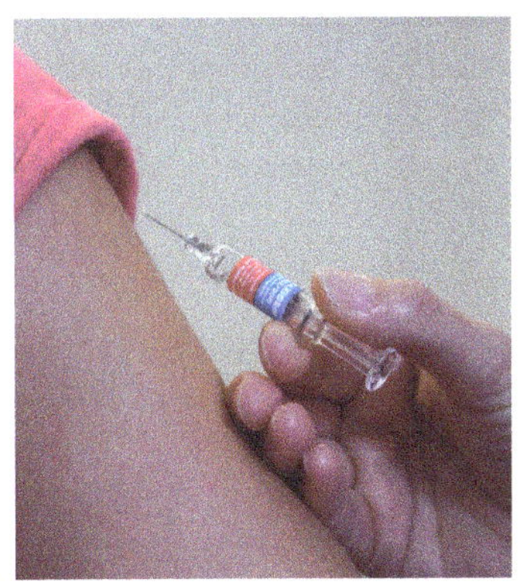

vaccination
vaksinasi

hospital
hospital

band aid
penampal luka

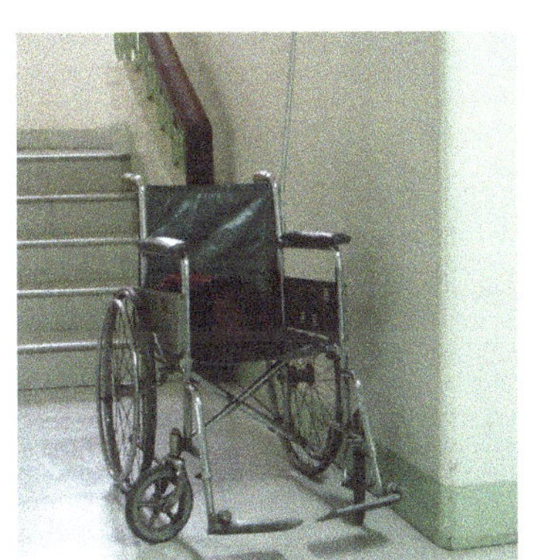

wheelchair
kerusi roda

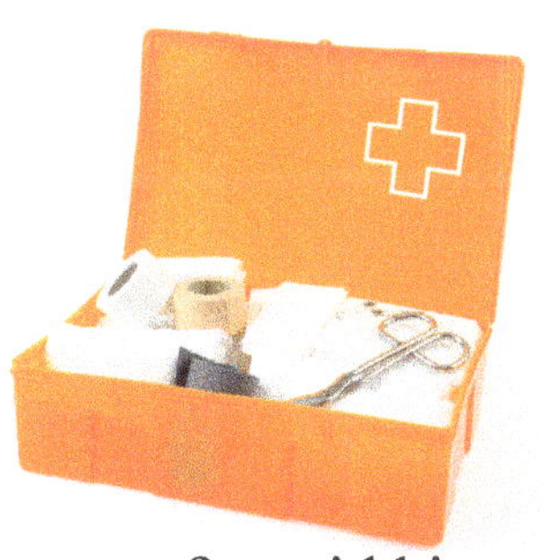

first aid kit
peti pertolongan cemas

pharmacy
farmasi

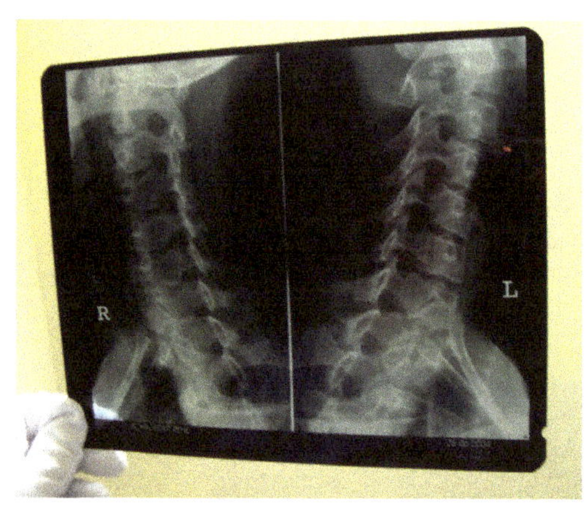

x-ray image
imej x-ray

thermometer
termometer

ambulance
ambulans

syringe
picagari

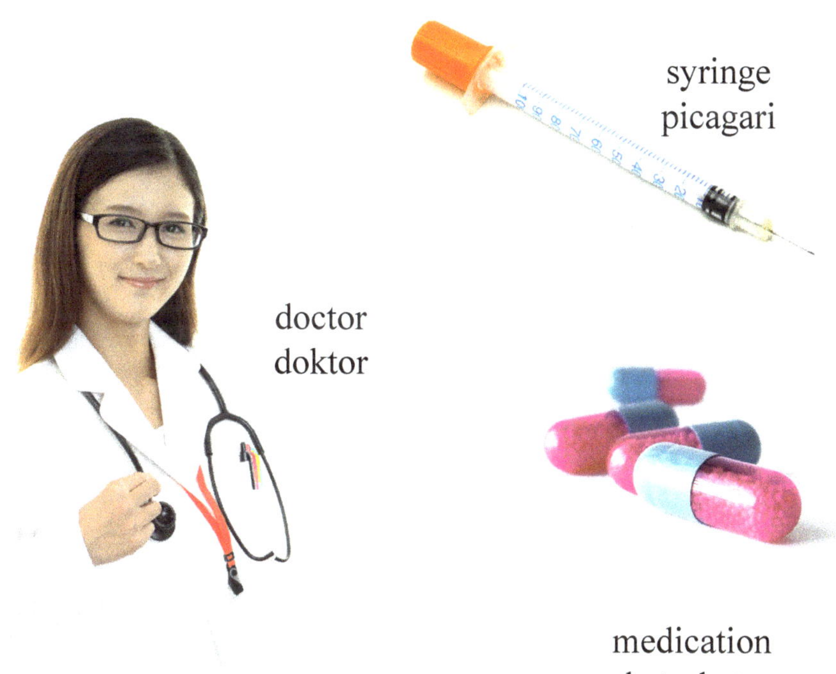

doctor
doktor

medication
ubat-ubatan

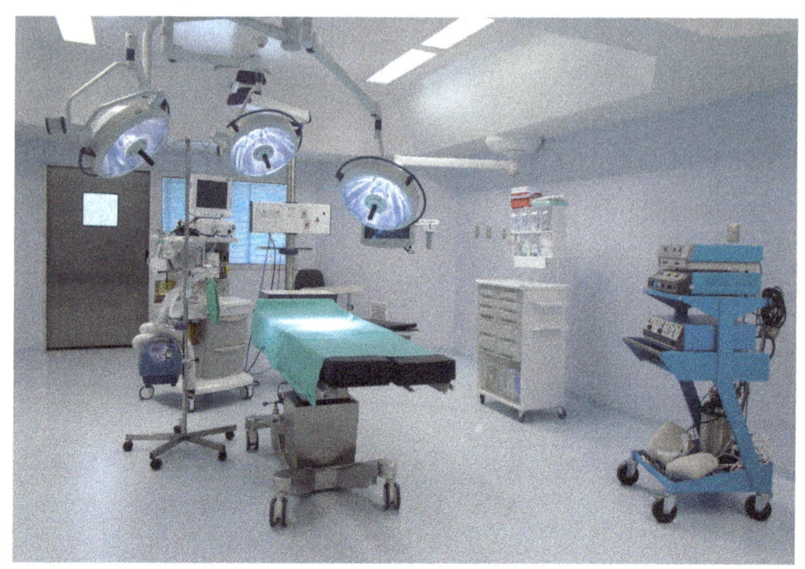

operating room
bilik pembedahan

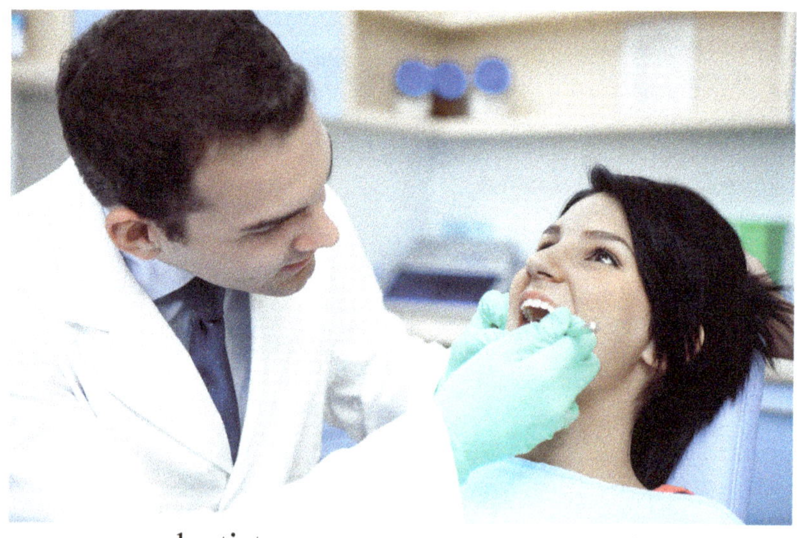

dentist   patient
doktor gigi   pesakit

to eat
makan

to drink
minum

to sit
duduk

to walk
berjalan

to talk
berbual

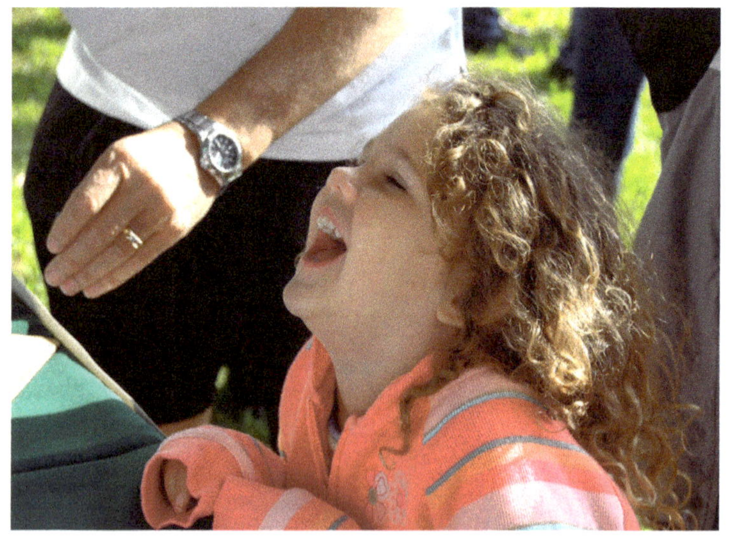

to laugh
ketawa

to carry
membawa

to stand
berdiri

to smile
senyum

to clean
membersih

to cook
memasak

to sneeze
bersin

to cry
menangis

to hug
memeluk

to sleep
tidur

to jump
melompat

to run
berlari

to swim
berenang

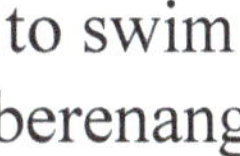

to read
membaca

to teach
mengajar

to play
bermain

to write
menulis

firefighter
bomba

florist
penjual bunga

musician
pemuzik

cleaner
tukang cuci

photographer
jurugambar

farmer
petani

artist
artis

chef
tukang masak

waitress
pelayan

teacher
guru

hairdresser
pendandan rambut

reporter
wartawan

bus driver
pemandu bas

librarian
pustakawan

square
segi empat sama

triangle
segi tiga

rectangle
segi empat tepat

circle
bulat

ellipse
bujur

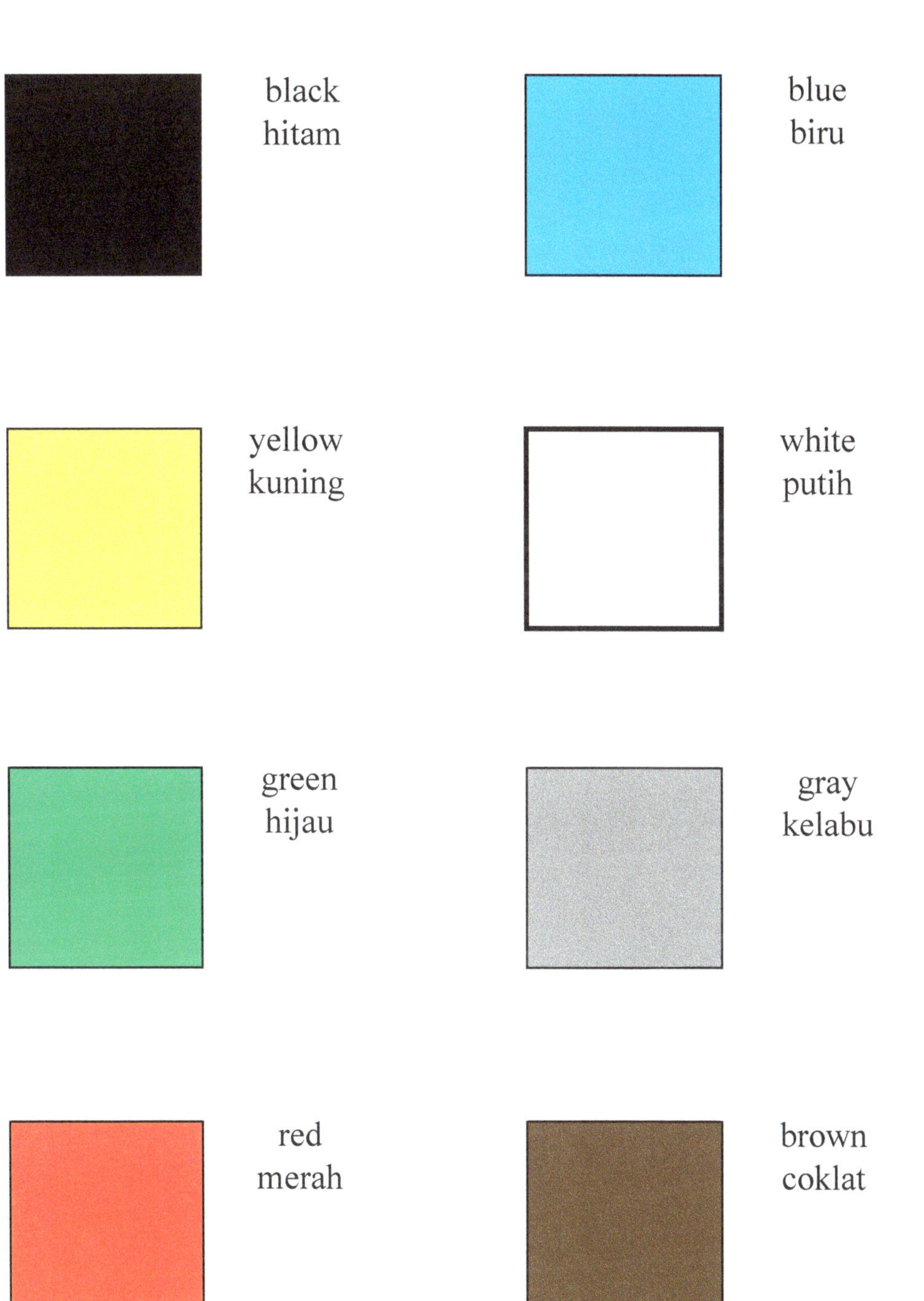
black
hitam
blue
biru
yellow
kuning
white
putih
green
hijau
gray
kelabu
red
merah
brown
coklat

happy
gembira

angry
marah

uncertain
tidak pasti

surprised
terkejut

confused
keliru

supportive
menyokong

thoughtful
berfikir

doubtful
ragu-ragu

big
besar

small
kecil

fast
laju

slow
perlahan

good
baik

bad
rosak

light
ringan

heavy
berat

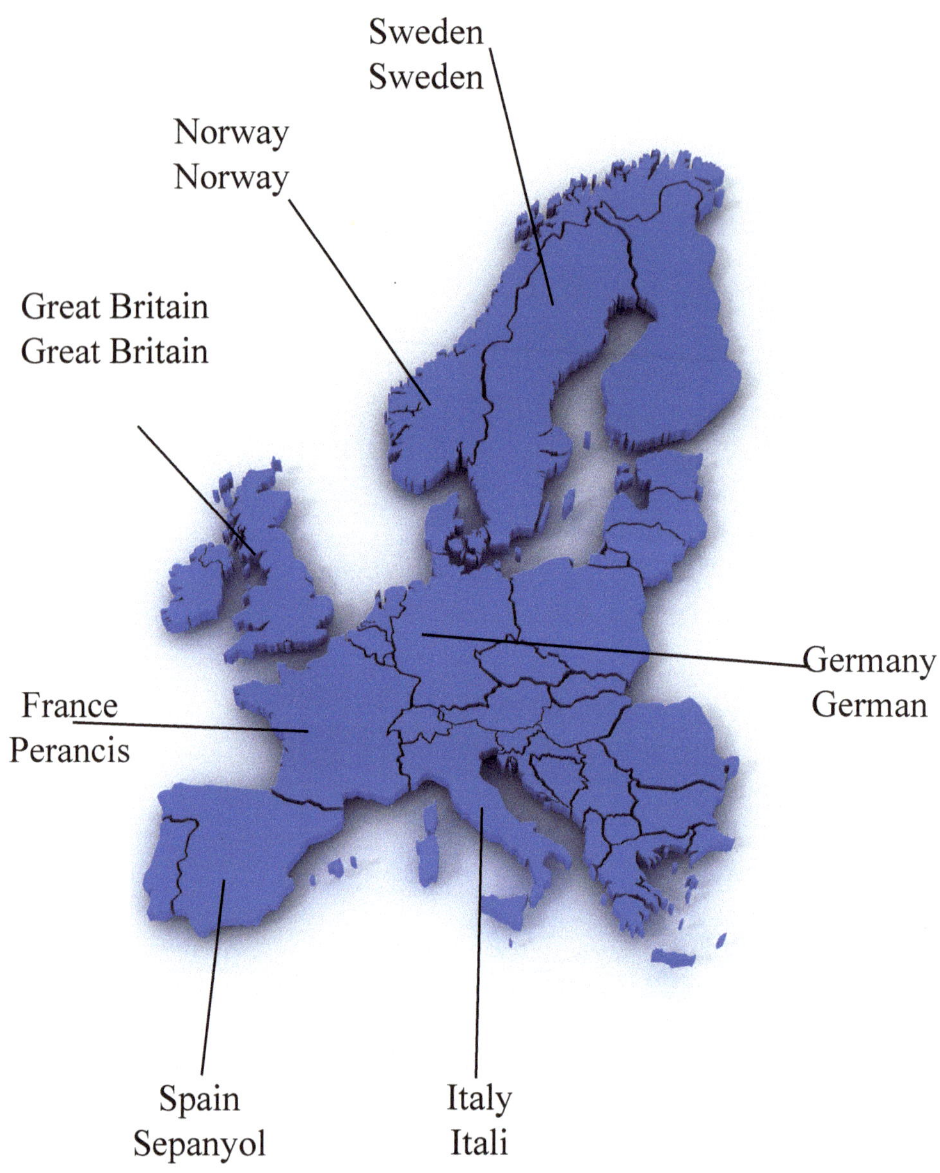

Sweden
Sweden
Norway
Norway
Great Britain
Great Britain
Germany
German
France
Perancis
Spain
Sepanyol
Italy
Itali

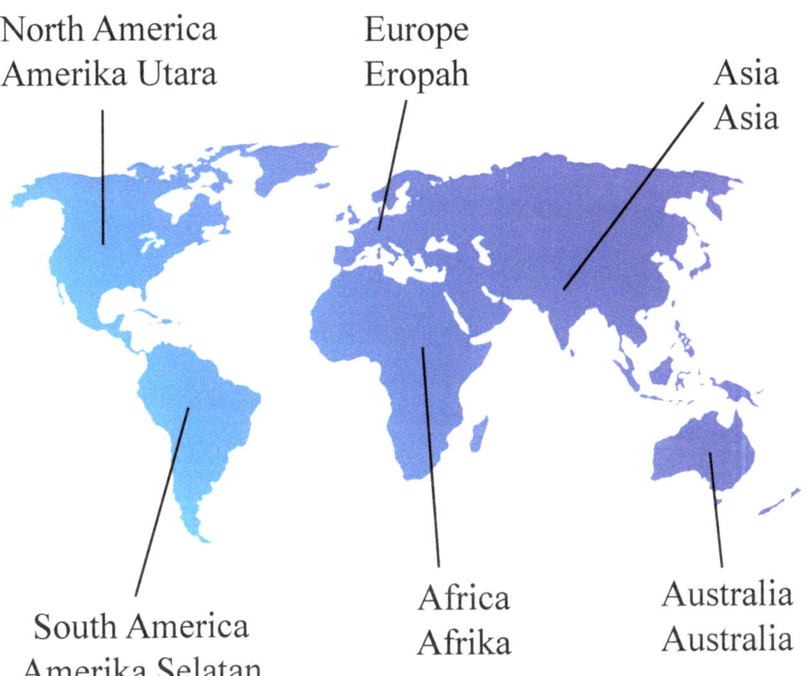
North America
Amerika Utara
Europe
Eropah
Asia
Asia
South America
Amerika Selatan
Africa
Afrika
Australia
Australia

spring
musim bunga

summer
musim panas

autumn
musim luruh

winter
musim salji